Why Elections Are The Problem

And

How to Make Democracy Real

An essay by

David Grant

© 2012

David W. Grant

CONTENTS

In the early 1980's I learned that the democracy of ancient Greece used a method altogether different than balloting to select its officials. They used the same system we use to select juries. Ever since then I have reflected upon how the lessons from that original democracy might be used to improve existing governance systems.

During the intervening decades, disaffection and distaste for politics and politicians have reached proportions great enough to demand fundamental review of this two hundred and twenty-five year old structure. I hope this article stimulates that review to begin.

*** The Problem ***

The problem, it would seem, stems from the fact that money controls politics. In more than 90% of elections for the House of Representatives and more than 80% of elections for the Senate, the candidate with the most money wins.[i] The contests are largely about controlling the agenda and, in that, sheer volume usually is all that matters. Yes, other factors come into play – connections and alliances through family, school, business and especially media – but 'the mother's milk of politics,' money, is the bald base of it.

Uncoupling the link between money and the requisites of electioneering is a no-brainer. With economic power seamlessly synchronized with political power — and reforms fashioned by those who are lock, stock and barrel invested in the system — 'campaign finance reform' can be nothing but a contradiction in terms.

But money is not the only thing. Winning an election also requires media presence, rhetorical flourish, expensive advertising and a personal characteristic so fundamental it is rarely acknowledged — namely, the willingness to compete against another human being. Electioneering demands playing a nasty game of one-upmanship. This means that the legislature is necessarily composed of a very small segment of the population – one that is psychologically more combative. Theories of conspiratorial power elites can be disregarded. Just note the psychological profile required. Since the great majority of people are different than that, it is obvious that elected legislatures can never be legitimate likenesses of all the people.[ii]

This is not to say that many representatives are not hard working, honest people doing their best to work for the good of all. Some certainly are that. But none of them are like the vast majority who would not ever choose to go through the campaign requirements of the rhetorical battles, the pandering for money, the unavoidable necessity to make shaky promises and generally to avoid being fully forthright. This means that there has never been, and never will be, a representation that is 'representational.'

It is furthermore gravely misleading to cheer that, thanks to the centuries long struggle to gain universal suffrage, the entire populace is in the happy position of being able to enter a booth once every few years in order to pull one lever or another. A true democracy requires equitable distribution of actual power, not merely the distribution of the 'consent' to be governed.

The United States was once the world's laboratory for democracy. Unbeknownst to most of its citizens, it has become the world's museum of democracy.

Museum, 17th Century

More than half the world's nations use some type of proportional representation.[iv] Some use more equitable and more accurate systems of voting.[v] U.S. election standards fail miserably to meet international norms.[vi] It isn't often mentioned in this country, but other nations have made political strides forward that we have not.

4

*** The Original ***

There is one major well-attested historical example of
thoroughgoing direct democracy. For about two hundred years,
Athens and other Greek city-states employed 'people power'
(*demos*, the people; *kratia*, power) to run its affairs. It is
worthwhile to look in some detail at how and why they did so.

Although Solon is credited as Greek's first 'lawgiver' it was not
until about fifty years after his death – 507/8 BCE – that the
reformer Cleisthenes established Athenian democracy. An
important support for this reform came from the rowers of the
triremes in Athens' formidable navy. Those rowers were not
galley slaves. They were free male citizens, 120 to 150 men per
ship. With democracy, they finally had a say in what had
previously been an autocracy.

Rowers in Athenian trireme

The new democrats did not exclude their richest 1%, but neither
did they hand them any more power than the same one vote that
every other man had who made it to the Assembly. When it
came to choosing office holders, elections were held only for

the posts of military and financial officials. The Athenian democrats chose their magistrates, their juries and their whole administrative apparatus by random selection of ordinary citizens. 'Random selection' is properly known as *sortition* — from the Latin: 'to divide, obtain or *sort* by lot.'

No doubt, socio-cultural differences between today and 2,500 years ago make comparisons of governmental systems intricate and fraught. One definition pointed to as irreconcilable is that of 'citizen.' Athenian 'citizens' composed only about 10% of the population. [viii] In its strict divisions of labor, women, slaves and foreigners were restricted to other duties.

Olive picking, a slave occupation [ix]

It is, of course, facile and foolish to tut-tut that gravely truncated right of suffrage. It only takes mentioning that at the time of the 1787 Constitution: women could not vote, slaves were enumerated as 3/5ths of a person, and American Indians not at all.

Wounded Knee massacre, aftermath[x]

For two hundred years Greek city-states organized themselves as either democracies or as oligarchies. Athens was the largest and by far best documented of the democracies. The record is clear that democratic Athens produced a stronger and more efficient system than any of its oligarchic neighbors. The preeminent scholar of democratic Greece, Mogens Herman Hansen, names five pillars of the Athenian system: 1.) belief in the intelligence of ordinary citizens; 2.) belief that ordinary citizens are prepared to disregard their self interest in case of conflict with the national interest; 3.) confidence that ordinary citizens can be kept sufficiently informed about the issues at stake; 4.) belief that ordinary citizens are interested in making decisions instead of delegating politics to professional representatives; 5.) support for amateurism insofar as common sense is considered sufficient to make rational decisions based upon the presentation of expert knowledge.[xi]

There were three parts to the Athenian government, but it is important to note from the outset that they are only partially analogous with the familiar tripartite of executive, legislative and judicial. The three bodies in Athens were the Assembly, the courts and a Council of 500. The Assembly met in the open air, about forty times a year, in an area called 'Pynx' that could hold up to 6,000 of Athens' 30,000 qualified voters.

The Pynx, meeting place of The Assembly

It was in the Assembly that direct democracy was used to vote for or against proposals. If you wanted to vote you had to get there before the place filled up. There was no concept of 'representation,' no concern about 'constituencies.' When it came to decisions about proposals, every man relied upon his own judgment. The actual vote was taken by the raise of hands. Since counting 6,000 hands was impractical, it was left to eyeballing by designated officials.[xiv]

All major political decisions were made by ordinary citizens in the Assembly or in law courts and legislative committees. These courts and committees were composed of those same ordinary citizens, chosen by lot. The juries were randomly selected on the day of trial. Jury size varied, depending on severity of the charges, from a minimum of 201 citizens up to 1,501 and at

8

least once to 6,001. The trials lasted only one day and had no judge or attorneys. The litigants made their own accusations and defense. After hearing the evidence, juries voted secretly and without deliberation. There were no appeals.

In order to make these decisions intelligent and informed, all proceedings, proposals and outcomes were published. This was a crucially important innovation. Previously the laws made by the aristocratic systems were communicated only verbally and only among the leaders. To make democracy work, a high degree of transparency was essential.

The work of the Council of 500 was to set the agenda for the Assembly and to oversee execution of the Assembly's decisions in the daily affairs of the city. The Council was not a legislative body. It was composed of citizens at least 30 years old who had volunteered to be placed in the lot for random selection. They served one-year terms and could be chosen no more than twice in a lifetime. The Council's leadership of 50 was sortitionally-chosen from among the 500. Those 50 led for only one month before being replaced by another sortitioned 50. The Council met every day except for festivals or days of ill omen. It examined the honesty and loyalty of other public officials, most of whom served for one year. It heard some impeachment cases. The Council of 500 was the state's bureaucracy but its ability to initiate was severely restricted. At the beginning, service was voluntary but later pay was instituted, making it easier for poorer citizens to volunteer.

If the Assembly felt the Council of 500 was not doing its duty, it could revoke and recall. The Assembly could also exile people – not only wrong doers but citizens who simply became too powerful or who had convinced the Assembly by power of oratory into bad decision. There was an elaborate system of forceful, administrative oversight. One could be severely fined or exiled for making what we today would call mere miscalculation or bad advice. Volunteering to be placed in the lot was not a thoughtless matter. Consequences of sanction could be grave.

The most famous critique of direct democracy came from the Athenian philosophers themselves. Both Plato and Aristotle claimed that, since the majority are always the poor, the poor would soak the rich. They expected 'the people' would confiscate property in the legal suits for which juries were sortitionally-selected. Evidence shows that although this may have occasionally occurred, the sortitionally-selected juries almost always gave a fair verdict to rich and poor alike.[xv]

xvi

The Death of Socrates

On the other hand, one of the Assembly's juries condemned Socrates to death. And contrary to popular conceptions that democracies are less bellicose, the Athenians waged imperial wars upon many of their neighbors.[xvii]

The criticisms come in hindsight. The thing that Athenians were most proud of was the fact that every citizen had the right to speak up and make proposals for laws and decrees. ('Voice equality' is the term proposed below in 'The Contemporary Option'.) They valued amateurism, fearing that if experts or professionals were given preference, they would take over. The driving force behind this system was that rotation of office insured that every citizen would, at some time in his life, rule over all the others. Rotation of office and amateurism were antidotes to corruption, cronyism and the cancer of factions. The idea was not only fear of retribution, should one lord it over another. The idea was also more benign. It was felt that only by experiencing obedience could one also command. There was reciprocity in it.

There were, nonetheless, fundamental differences between leaders and followers. This was partly because of simple physical logistics. Although all of the 6,000 who could cram into the Pynx had the right to speak, if everyone did the Assembly would have been impossible. The space constraint also meant that at most only 1 out of 5 citizens could attend.[xviii] Naturally, there were some few with expert knowledge to contribute along with the many who brought only the common sense to listen and to choose between proposals submitted.

The democratic Greeks did not, however, use sortition to choose their treasurers or their generals. When scholars speak of Pericles as the 'leader' of the later period of democratic Athens – and associate him with power 'like a president's', or even 'like a dictator's' — it was the power of his oratory, coupled with his repeated election (as one of the generals), that he was recognized.[xix] But other than those few meritocratic positions, the Athenians did choose – as astounding as it may seem — all other administrative, judicial and executive office holders by sortition.[xx]

Even though there was social pressure upon all free male citizens to take part in political activity, records indicate that many participated willingly. Most took pride in fulfilling their service in the many administrative functions. They seemed to derive actual enjoyment from the debates and the decisions in the Assembly. To take part in the dialectical struggles was a positive value.[xxi] There were, though, some who did not relish or take an active part. The word applied to them in that first democracy 2,500 years ago was *idiot*. The literal translation means 'private person' – in context: one who fails to fulfill his duty as a citizen to govern the city. As said, the cultural gulf between then and now makes it foolhardy to claim unmitigated transference of 'the original' democracy to contemporary circumstances. Nonetheless exemplary aspects of that original should be studied and modified for use today.

After the conquest of Greece by Alexander of Macedonia and final Athenian defeat in 322 BCE, the institution of democracy lay dormant for most of two thousand years. Monarchs and tyrants didn't like it. Eventually, in the late medieval period and Renaissance, aristocratic factions in Italian city-states were bleeding each other so ferociously that they picked up sortitional selection as a means of eliminating their feuds.[xxii] Later on in colonial New England, Open Town Meetings[xxiii] developed similarities with the Athenian Assembly. Today in Switzerland, two cantons still hold annual open air sessions where all citizens assemble to make legally-binding decisions. But these examples were not designed based on knowledge of Athens. They are examples of the many historical instances of independent, sometimes simultaneous, invention or discovery. More than a hundred years have passed, for instance, since the airplane was invented twice — at the same time and on two continents. [xxiv] As far as airplanes of today are concerned, the lessons of those earliest antecedents are so deeply ingrained and surpassed that they are themselves no longer of design consequence.

The 'first flight' – Santos-Dumont, 1906

In the same way, the historical alternative presented by study of the original democracy makes moot the question: "Is direct democracy possible?" Not only can we be assured that real democracy is possible, we can envision and confidently work towards a near future of broader democratic vistas.

American civics classes teach that Classical Athens was the progenitor of democracy and that voting was the core of its practice. As a result, most Americans believe elections and democracy are the same.[xxvi] But, as we have seen, in that first democracy voting was used mostly to accept or to reject policies or legal judgments. Aristotle put it bluntly: "It is accepted as democratic when public offices are allocated by lot; and as oligarchic [rule by the few] when they are filled by election."[xxvii] In the American system, sortition is used only to select juries.

The founders of the American republic were men of the middle and upper classes. They knew about the practice of sortition in Athens, though not in detail. Enamored of ideas from the European Enlightenment, particularly John Locke's 'natural law theory,' when they sought models, they did not choose Athens. They chose as their governmental model: Rome.[xxviii] The Roman Senate was 'representative', yes, and thus a 'republic,' but property qualifications limited participation to aristocrats.

Even though the Founding Fathers admired and incorporated Montesquieu's ideas about checks and balances, they ignored that he wrote: "Selection by lot is in the nature of democracy, selection by choice [election] is in the nature of aristocracy. The lot is a way of selecting that offends no one; it leaves to each citizen a reasonable expectation of serving his country".[xxix] The American founders dismissed the idea because their battle was against the rights of heredity. It was not about solicitude for the commonweal. When James Madison emulated Montesquieu's 'checks and balances' with a tripartite system, he was creating bulwarks against democracy's Achilles heel – the tyranny of the majority.

Tar-and-feathering

The founders feared ochlocracy – mob rule.[xxxi]

Not that the American founders were conspiring against 'true democracy.' They did not have to 'conspire' since they knew that a popular vote would insure control by the upper classes.[xxxii] The groundwork had been laid in the late 1600's by the 'Father of Classical Liberalism', John Locke. He formulated the notion of 'consent of the governed' — which is to say the 'consent' to be ruled.[xxxiii] It had nothing to do with control of actual power by the general populace. Writing about the proposed Congress, Alexander Hamilton put it plainly: "... the representative body ... will be composed of landholders, merchants and men of the learned professions. Where is the danger," Hamilton wrote, "that the interests and feelings of the different classes of citizens will not be understood or attended to by these three descriptions of men?"[xxxiv] Even though generally opposed to Hamilton, Thomas Jefferson wrote in a similar vein in 1813 to John Adams: "[T]here is a natural aristocracy among men. The grounds of this are virtue and talents. [...] May we not even say that that form of government is the best which provides the most effectually for a pure selection of these natural *aristoi* ['aristocracy,' Greek] into the offices of government?"[xxxv]

No doubt the American founders made political strides by overpowering hereditary monarchy. What they did with that power was to extend it to "landholders, merchants and men of the learned professions".[xxxvi] Despite the fact that a significant faction of the constitutional framers – the 'Anti-Federalists' – did want to see representative actually reflect the full make-up

16

of the population, they could not unfortunately envision the sortitional mechanism that could extend it to all sectors of society.

As much as we may be astonished to learn that the Athenian democracy used sortition to choose its office holders, it is perhaps even more surprising to learn that, until 170 years ago, 'democracy' and 'representation' were considered opposing and irreconcilable forms of government. 'People power' was diametrically opposed to 'representation,' understood to be that aristocratic form of republican Rome.[xxxvii]

[xxxviii]

The Roman Forum

It was not until Alexis de Tocqueville published his *Democracy in America* in the late 1830's that 'representative democracy' entered our nomenclature.[xxxix] What is often overlooked in the references to that famous cheerleader for early American 'democracy' is that he was not writing about the elitist perceptions of the original founders. Tocqueville travelled in the U.S. in 1831-32 when Andrew Jackson had broken with the aristocratic paradigm. Jackson had jumped on a populist bandwagon that raised the utterly novel banner of *representative* democracy.[xl] Before Jackson, 'representation' was bald oligarchy — rule by the few, the landed, the elite. Before Jackson, voters (Euro-American males) generally ignored politics in deference to the realm of that 'natural *aristoi.*' Jeffersonian democracy may have opposed inherited elites but it favored the educated. Jacksonians shifted that emphasis by appealing to the common man with mass meetings, parades and celebrations which generated intense enthusiasm and, for the first time in America, high voter participation.[xli] One could say that Tocqueville denominated a new hybrid when he reported that 'democracy' – the direct popular franchise which, for almost two thousand years, had been largely despised and dismissed — was now united with its former oppositional type. 'Democracy' was now interpreted as possible by 'representation.'

When presented with the option of randomly selecting representatives to a 'Citizen Legislature' (as posited by Callenbach and Philips, 1985)[xlii] many people dismiss the proposal out of hand as absurd. When the argument is buttressed with the example of sortition's extensive role in the original Athenian democracy — and the fact that voting for candidates inherently creates oligarchy – such a person will often need a breath to recover from ideological shock. Only when they are reminded that selecting a jury of one's peers depends upon random selection of ordinary citizens will they seriously entertain the pros and cons. Soon they then bring up concerns about competence, about corruption and about accountability.

About competence, the first thing to note is, again, the jury. Long ago we decided that citizens of general and average intelligence are competent to make judgments of guilt or innocence. Sometimes of life or death.

Contemporary juries are not, however, formed only of the randomly selected. The purpose of the *voir dire* process (preliminary examination by judge or counsel) is meant to winnow out the patently incompetent or biased. Just so, the proposal for a sortitioned Citizen Legislature would require that those who wish to place themselves into the allotment pool should demonstrate a basic understanding of how the existing system of government works. Such a test should, however, ensure that the great majority of citizens would qualify. The naturalization test required of immigrants seeking citizenship would suffice as such a demonstration.[xliii] The pass rate on that exam is greater than the pass rate for the average driver's license test.[xliv]

Once selected, the new representatives would undergo substantial orientation to legislative and administrative procedures. They would choose their own professional staff as well as have access to all the resources of the current Congress. Three-year terms should be staggered so that freshmen compose one-third of every new session.

The question about competence then becomes "Is that good enough?"

Yes, it is. Not only good enough but better than anything any one person is likely to consciously devise. It is supremely rational in this case to choose an 'a-rational' way of choosing legislators.[xlv] Sources of information and the breadth of knowledge in a sortitionally-selected group will be greater and more diverse than among representatives chosen by election. Empirical evidence shows that decisions made by large diverse groups on non-technical issues have been proven superior to those made by professional experts. Most important of all, a Citizen Legislature will be psychologically heterogeneous. Instead of filtering representatives through the gauntlet of political campaign, ensuring only one type of representation – that of those aggressive enough and rich enough to promote one's own self – the full panoply of citizenry will actually wield power. The wisdom of everyday citizens is more than adequate.[xlvi]

Just as it has taken a while to acknowledge that 'women hold up half the sky,'[xlvii] we also need to acknowledge that so do all those who would <u>not</u> seek candidacy by election. We need everybody 'in.' Research indicates, by the way, that the inclusion in a group of some who are <u>not</u> well-informed about a topic generally increases overall sagacity of the group. The reason for this is that when 'well-informed' people are presented information contrary to opinions they have already formed, they often fail to remember the new facts. Cognitive dissonance is unpleasant. But when those who know nothing about the topic hear such information, they do not kneejerk and dismiss it.[xlviii]

In any case, this is not about the expertise needed to construct a rocket ship.

Apollo 11 boot print

Nor is it like man-on-the-street polling. Nor is it like suggestions that everyone can vote on everything via the internet. The Center for Deliberative Democracy has proven that the time — the leisure — to deliberate and to have access to full and complete information makes a sortitionally-selected legislature crucially different from polling or referenda.[l]

Even when it comes to technical matters, studies demonstrate that the presence of non-specialists among a group of experts significantly improves the solutions which the group may devise.[li] When experts are all in the same box, as they usually are, it makes sense to add to that group someone from outside of it. Diversity of views is protection against the group-think that can arise in any homogenous 'mob.'[lii] In a similar fashion, regarding the persuasive sway of a rhetorically adroit demagogue or of a determined fanatical clique — and counter to the civic ambition of participation by all – the presence of individuals with the least interest in a particular outcome can often induce salutary protection.[liii]

Once it is apparent that wise – indeed, <u>wiser</u> — decisions are assured by an amateur legislative 'jury', the question arises: Who will provide the information for deliberation? Or the contrary: How will disinformation be revealed? For the general public, media will always play an important role — whether boon or block. For more intensive deliberations, best efforts must be made to provide all competing positions on the policies under discussion.[liv] A Citizen Legislature will rely, just as the current Congress does, on professional staffs with access to the full range of governmental resources.

Concomitant to skepticism about sources of information is the query famously expressed by the Roman satirist Juvenal, "Who will guard the guardians?" How will these unelected legislative 'jurists' be held to account?

They will be held to account mostly by leaving things as they are. The checks and balances of executive, judicial and legislative will continue to operate in all their contentious, but ultimately effective, glory. Given that representatives in a Citizen Legislature will be beholden to no political parties, to no financial contributors, to no interest or advocacy groups, it should be expected that they will have no compunction about criticizing and condemning wrong doers. The existing Ethics Committee will provide tougher internal oversight than they do now because sortitionally-selected representatives will be much more heterogeneous than the current club. The courts and media and civil society all will continue 'watching' – even more so since all citizens will be invested. All are 'in.'

There is one unavoidable ironic development that comes along with attempting to establish a truly representative legislature. The moment that a representative is chosen, he or she will immediately lose 'representativeness' because she or he would no longer be one of the thousands who were not chosen. This distinction will rapidly increase as the representative body digests information that fellow citizens will not have. The representatives will also have much more time than the general population to deliberate. In comparison with the current system, they will have twice as much time since they will not be using half their time, as current Congress members must, to raise funds and campaign.

The Citizen Legislature would be equivalent to the General Assembly of Athens insofar as the Assembly was composed of only a small part of the population. Inevitably such a body is a sort of elite. But unlike the Athenian Assembly, the Citizen Legislature would contain all sectors of society. Further protection against this problem of legislative separation from the polis is the term limit. A more subtle and longer term democratizing effect will be the effective distribution of leadership experience far and wide. The local and regional effect will mean a polity more capable and more invested. It might even be that 'the government' is recognized as 'of and by' – as well as, as now, ostensibly, 'for' – the people.

It is often lamented today that citizens are apathetic or cynical. But the obvious truth is that failure to attend to public affairs does not mean that one is a lazy bum and an irresponsible citizen. It just means that one does not want to spend a lot of time in meetings, especially not in ones merely advisory for 'citizen input.' And when it comes to voting for candidates, there is a 'rational ignorance' in the decision not to spend a lot of time ferreting out what candidate made which promises most seductive to one's personal or communal ideals and interests. Not only is it rational to acknowledge that one's individual vote in a general election for a candidate has a statistically negligible influence, it is also rational to prioritize personal activities that are more exciting, more fun, more creative and more productive – for oneself as well as for the commonweal. This is another reason why creating a legislature that mirrors the full population is efficient, fair and smart.

To repeat, it is only voting for candidates that ceases. In the Citizen Legislature voting about policy matters continues full tilt. Direct democracy by one-person, one-vote remains the modus operandi of the legislative body. Since that body is sortitionally-chosen, it is proportional to as much of the general populace that volunteers and thus acts, in essence, as the full 'electorate.' Even so, one might wonder if the previously mentioned 'rational ignorance' might come into play in the

Citizen Legislature itself? At what point will a representative decide that the amount of time necessary to study a policy issue will not be worth the possibility of that representative's one vote having decisive effect? Specifically the question would be: "At what number does this effect take hold?" If one is one-out-of-five-hundred? Or one-out-of-five-thousand? Of course this question applies to the present 435 members of Congress and is often solved by party affiliation. A proportionally representative body would presumably respond in a similar fashion. They would listen to opinions of sympathetic cohorts, including political parties, lobbyists, advocates, the media and so on. Most importantly, they would carefully attend – one could say 'unavoidably' — to the views of the social and cultural circles from which they came.

Another critique applied to any representative body – whether Congress as it is or as it would be if sortitioned — is just how 'representative' can it be? How reflective of the general population? How proportional? A Congressional district is composed of about 600,000 people. Philosophically (ontologically), the only person that a human being can fully 'represent' is the person him- or herself.[lv] But even admitting that no one is truly 'unique,' one will always wonder: "Are there, indeed, 600,000 people who are sufficiently 'like me' so that I will be 'represented'?" And what if there are only 300,000 of whom a person would consider 'close enough'? In that case a legislature of 1,000 would be required. This question of "What is the right percentage?" was hotly debated at the Philadelphia Convention of 1787 and probably will be forever under scrutiny. Representation can never be anything but imperfect.

Still, the question remains: If the full spectrum of citizens were sitting in a sortitionally-selected Citizen Legislature would they be any less subject than current Congresses to corruption?

lvi

Bribery in cold cash

It might first be noted that a recent informal comparison was made between the rate of criminality of Congress and that of urban high crime neighborhoods. It was found that Congressional members broke the law about twice as often as do citizens in such neighborhoods.[lvii]

Although it may take a little time, power and the associated privileges will change almost anyone. The Greek democrats had a complicated system of checks and balances. They did not particularly trust each other. It was not always about the money. It could be, as it sometimes is today, about identity. "A sacred troth" may sound like an outmoded medievalism but it takes a mere moment's reflection to acknowledge that honor and pride can drive just as much mischief as greed, anger or lust.

The contemporary option to apply sortition is not equivalent to the way the Greeks used it. Their Assembly acted as judge, jury and executor. The contemporary proposal is about the legislature. Not the executive or the judiciary. Those positions should be filled based on merit.

Of course there will be technical matters that need to be understood. One might say that "even though it's not about rocket science, sometimes it is." Scientific matters can be daunting. But, again, the current Congress faces the same problem since there rarely are scientists in it. Any legislature will face specialized sectors spinning tales to justify their existence and it can be expected that entrenched bureaucracies will continue to pitch needs for ever-more funding. The strongest argument for long legislative tenure is that it increases incumbents' investigative savvy.[lviii] An experienced skeptical nose can smell and root out — sometimes only if politically advantageous — subterfuge and lies. The loss of institutional memory in a constantly rotating policy-making body is potentially a grave weakness. This will be an area that needs special attention. Civil society and independent media will need to carefully monitor and report. But, again, these challenges are not qualitatively different than posed in the current system. Like any other living system, a Citizen Legislature will continually adjust to, and be adjusted by, its circumstances.

So what would happen to political parties? The founding fathers had hoped to avoid their creation, but the hope was in vain. They feared that intransigent factions would employ any stratagem, including gridlock and even violent revolution, to block opponents for the sake of gaining or re-gaining power.[lix] With the sortitional selection of candidates, political parties would probably become smaller and more numerous. They would continue to advocate positions and platforms, but without the spoils of election, their power to set agendas would be much diminished. But not eliminated. (A proposed counterbalance to the inevitability of power elites is suggested in the next section.) Debates in the Citizen Legislature would be about issues that were raised by all segments of the population, not just by two large political parties. Although of course there will continue to be lobbyists and advocates for special interests — some good, some bad — sortition would insure 'voice equality'[lx] irrespective of economic or social class.

Although sortition foreseen in this proposal affects only the legislative branch there has been thought about how it might be extended to choosing the executive. Somewhat like in a parliamentary system, a Citizen Legislature could interview, hire and fire the executive. That would save the great expense and years of time devoted to presidential campaigns. Or a pool of candidates could go through popular election to reach a given threshold and then be selected by lot. This is similar to what went on for hundreds of years in some of the city-states of Renaissance Italy. It is also similar to how the Amish have, for a few centuries, chosen their theocratic leaders.[lxi]

It is beyond the scope of this paper to delve into the Theory of Emergence[lxii] as an explication of the evolutionary function of sortition. Suffice it to say that the more that 'everybody's in' — the more that full voice equality is brought to bear — the more quickly and completely will humanity, as a self-aware species, realize whatever its endowed potential is destined to be.

Protecting "life, liberty and the pursuit of happiness" is a tall order. It is a tall order even if 'happiness' is taken to mean, as it once was, 'property.'[lxiii] Happiness consists not only of the material senses of food, habitation and sex, but also the intangibles of love, knowledge and beauty. When it comes to communal happiness, social relationships require cognition, cooperation and coordination. Good institutions help make good citizens. Happy ones as well.

Happiness and inclusiveness are inextricable. The most consequential aspect of the argument for sortitional, not elective, selection of policy-making bodies is that it is only through random selection that all willing and able citizens gain an equal opportunity to actually make policy. The Law of Large Numbers assures, statistically, that those chosen by random selection will proportionally represent the population from which they are selected.[lxiv] The proportions achieved through random selection at large-scale will reliably mirror the body politic.[lxv]

Another concomitant of happiness is fairness. What, for instance, would be adequate compensation for the once-in-a-lifetime service in a Citizen Legislature?

[lxvi]

Stone money

31

Perhaps a salary at the 90th percentile of average household income would be enough to mitigate disruption to one's livelihood.[lxvii] That would be about $83,000, close to one half of the $174,000 Congressmen make today. Such a salary would also encourage most people to register for the lot. Only the top 10% would be 'losing money' by accepting the call to civic duty.

By this time in this essay, many readers will hopefully be saying "This is a good idea." It is also likely that such readers will immediately add "…but it has a snowball's chance in hell of ever happening." To such skeptics, here are two of many rejoinders. First, from Mohandas Gandhi: "First they ignore you; then they laugh at you; then they fight you; then you win." Second, more recently and street-generic: "It's got no more chance than electing a Kansan-Kenyan with an African name for President." With the shortcomings of money-influenced elections as widely recognized and as severe as they are (to say nothing of election's other inherently inequitable functions), the only known remedy – the mechanism most widely used by that very first democracy – must be comprehensively employed.

Of course there will be resistance. Professional politicians have already legally shut down moderate versions of proportional representation.[lxviii] The technologic and economic paradigms that promote efficiencies through division of labor have so aggrandized the concept of professionalism that anything deemed amateur is dismissed as unworthy and second-rate. Overweening professionalism ossifies into habits often unrelated to the matters at hand. Amateurs act with the strength of loving what they do.

Fortunately, some entities are implementing sortition for political matters. Here are some examples.

In the State of Washington, the Commission on Salaries for Elected Officials is composed of nine citizens randomly-selected and seven appointed. Every two years, the commission determines the salaries of almost five hundred elected state officials.[lxix]

In Oregon, the Citizens' Initiative Review is a panel of randomly-selected and demographically-balanced voters brought together to fairly evaluate ballot measures. They publish a voters' pamphlet of their most important findings. It is in effect a deliberation done by a proportionally representative jury of voting citizens.[lxx]

California is sometimes presented as a negative example of what can happen with citizen initiatives. Big money is required to gather the large number of signatures necessary to place a measure on the ballot. Advertising can override considered deliberation. But a recent pilot 'Deliberative Initiative' in California, using randomly selected citizens, shows that direct democracy can be successfully practiced without commercial distortions. The initiative brings transparency and accountability to the state's budget process and ensures local control of some services.[lxxi]

In a Citizen Assembly held in British Columbia, a randomly selected group went through an extensive process of deliberating about electoral reform.[lxxii] After holding many public hearings and listening to the experts, they came up with a plan to increase proportional representation.[lxxiii] But when the plan was put to a province-wide referendum, only 55% approved, not enough to reach the 60% threshold. Research showed that when people fully understood the proposal, they supported it. But there were many un-informed voters. This highlights the difference between mere polling and concerted deliberation. It strengthens the case for a fully empowered Citizen Legislature without requirement of further mass ratification.

In Australia a new initiative hands a municipality's $74 million budget to a few dozen sortitionally-selected citizens. After extensive deliberation and public hearings, they will recommend service levels and funding models for the next four years. The city council will give its final approval, or not, without the ability to modify or amend. The city councilors agreed to this scheme because they saw that such a group would de-politicize the process and provide greater credibility to the outcome.[lxxiv]

'Making democracy real' will necessarily extend more broadly. Sortition and direct democracy can be used not only in the political arena but also in schools, clubs, sports, corporate committees and wherever voice equality is required.[lxxv] Other contemporary examples that have used sortition in whole or in part include village assemblies in Bhutan[lxxvi]; the board of a nonprofit group[lxxvii]; Danish 'consensus conferences'; the South Australian Constitutional Convention; the Internet Engineering Task Force; Spanish savings banks for electing representatives of account holders; election monitors and ballot counters in Switzerland, Argentina and Spain.[lxxviii]

Democracy has two legs: voting and sortition. The distinction between balloting for policy and sortitioning for candidates is crucial to this proposition. All the more so in an age of mass media and the impossibility of face-to-face contact with candidates. Elections for meritocratic office holders might be best used for selecting among candidates at local and small-scale.[lxxix] Voting for a candidate one has personally met is certainly more satisfying than voting for an image.

The vision presented in this article is of a fully sortitional Citizen Legislature. That is the end goal. It would be reckless to institute it full blown. Best would be a well-designed gradual transition to reduce the risk of catastrophic unintended consequences. It can begin, as it already has, in small municipalities. Then it can move to provincial or state level. Then to a full Citizen Legislature. Some are even considering how it might be applied at the United Nations.[lxxx]

Another gradualist approach is to apply sortitional committees to specific issues — first one issue, then more, then to all issues. In a municipality such a committee would ensure that a particular decision would not be fashioned, as they so often are, by a small self-serving group. A first trial of such a sortitioned panel could be for a simple, short-term decision — such as allocation of funds for a year to re-pave streets. Once comfortable with that experience, a municipality could use the methodology for more complicated issues – such as the decision to build a new sports stadium with 40-year bonds. Such a panel would need to be larger and with a remit to institute wide public deliberation.

Another example of gradualist implementation would be to increase the degrees of power of sortitionally-selected bodies — first only as advisory; then with limited enforcement capacity (such as the ability to force votes that are stuck in committee; or a veto power); finally to full legislative powers. Yet another approach would be to begin with only a few members of a policy-making body selected sortitionally, then more, then finally all.[lxxxi]

Since elections have so long been the only standard for forming governments, some fear – but also some welcome — sortition as a radical upending of tradition. In either case, manipulation by elites is a concern. The existing elites will seek to maintain their positions. The 'up-enders' will seek to replace them. In order to address the fact that elites (whether by education, rhetoric or finance) always seem to slip through loopholes, some propose that it would be best to recognize their inevitable influence and leave the upper chamber as it is — as an elected Senate[lxxxii]. In that case, these elites would remain banded together in their political parties and could continue to spend all the money they want to get themselves elected. Those who argue this say that by otherwise attempting to ban them, these elites will just be driven underground. Political parties, the argument goes, are easier to police than the mafia.

In such a scenario, the elected Senate would be the place where bills are formulated and introduced. The sortitioned House would be the place in which those bills are approved or rejected. It would be like the example in which two children must divide a cake. The one who cuts the cake only gets to choose his or her piece after the one who doesn't. That insures that the one cutting will accurately divide the piece equally. The proposal to retain an elected Senate retains the assumption that there will always be elites — 'the aristoi' identified by Jefferson. Finally, any proposal that entirely disenfranchises (so to speak) politicians formerly used to being elected will be unlikely to garner the support needed – short of violent uprising — to put any new sortitional regimen into place.

The riposte to this idea of maintaining a special venue for the elite is that the point of choosing by sortition is to say that we are all in this together, that there is no us-versus-them, no selfish aristocracy versus the unwashed masses. And that therefore one unicameral sortitionally-selected legislature is all that is needed, is fair and just.[lxxxiii]

Even though "...*We hold these truths to be self-evident, that all men are created equal...*" the fact is that all are not born equal. Not in wealth, not in skills, aptitude, intelligence, physical abilities ... many things. But we have accepted that we are all born equally human. The discourse about how to maintain this equality of humanness can only be satisfied under the principle of 'voice equality.' Sortition is not a leftist or a rightist idea. It welcomes the spectrum from beyond the Tea Party to beyond the Occupy Movement.

The impetus to insure full voice equality – the next great step after the accomplishment of universal suffrage – may require long, slow evolution. On the other hand, many far-reaching social changes have occurred with rapidity and surprise – the end of the Cold War and the more recent Arab Spring, just two examples of many. In any case, there are three final obstacles, perhaps the most formidable, that are less obvious than all those previously listed.

Inertia. Fear. And reasonableness.

Inertia affects everything. Everyone rightly values stability in most areas of their lives so as to focus on priorities, whatever they may be. Inertia, though, has turned the U.S. into the world's museum of democracy because inertia has us still sitting on the laurels of 1776 and 1787.

Fear, as Franklin Roosevelt said, is the only thing worthy of itself. To put trust in each other does indeed require a certain fearlessness. But it need not require blind faith in the goodness of all. By using sortition there is no 'trust' necessary to expect equal distribution of power. Distributive equality through sortition is simply assured. It just 'happens'…without human agency, without human conniving. Let it be tried on various levels and then judge it on its practicality and on its merits.

Why finally, you might ask, is reasonableness an impediment?

Because reasonableness by itself lacks drama, lacks fire. Dispassionate argument speaks only to the intellect. For many: 'boring.'

Human nature loves the fire. Humans are hard-wired to be curious. Humans are hardwired to seek the edge, the ferment, the fight. Humans are fundamentally creatures who like to 'play.'[lxxxiv] Little wonder that the media heightens the competitive nature of elections, treating them as sporting events. It is not that the media seeks only what is commercially lucrative. It is that they feed our inherent desire to play. Sortition removes the electoral fray. With sortition the over-heated political arena might just de-populate. Sortition is such a rational and egalitarian idea that one can worry it may not ignite the emotional conviction requisite for major social change.

Inspiration is needed. Speeches, essays, novels, movies, poems and performances are needed. Common Lot Productions, of which the author is president, aims to contribute in this arena.[lxxxv]

In response to this last formidable obstacle — dispassionate reasonableness — readers might want to reprise a scene from the movie *Network*. In this scene the disgruntled, embittered anchorman of the broadcast news program urges viewers nationwide to go to the window, open it, stick out their heads and yell their frustration: "I'm mad as hell and I'm not going to take it anymore!"[lxxxvi] Only this time many readers will be using a mobile device and may be in public space already. Stand by, then, dear reader, to Get Up And Testify!

Practice discretely at first.

Quietly, to yourself … Let me hear you say "Amen!"

A little louder, please.

"Amen!"

All right. We're ready now.

Brothers and sisters, we've got to work together, play together, protect each other.

Say it out loud now: "Amen!"

Oligarchs have stolen the concept, the very concept, of democracy. We've got to take it back!

Say it louder: "Amen!"

The road to self-governance has too long been strewn with boulders of disinformation, deception, obfuscation and skullduggery. Democracy is not merely about fair distribution of <u>consent</u>. It is about fair distribution of <u>actual, real, citizen power</u>!

Shout it out! "Amen!"

We want to struggle together, to come the right decisions together, sit at the table of our one human family together. We want to talk it out with each other.

All of us, each and every one of us. With full voice equality.

Testify! Don't hold back!

"Amen, brothers and sister!"

"Amen, our dear children of the future!"

"Amen! Amen! Amen!"

We won't all agree. Some of us may sit off to the side on some things.

"Yes, some may sit it out."

(Quietly, now, building steam for finale…)

No need to worry that voice equality will mean no more struggle, no more battle, no more 'play.' It won't be boring.

(Throw in a chuckle.)

But if we will just take the time to listen to each other…

"Amen!"

Pay respect to each other.

"Preach!"

We can transcend our petty differences.

And to that, we all can say it one more time —

"Amen!"

======= AMEN =======

APPENDIX A

RESOURCES

[including some listed in end notes]

Author's website

Common Lot Productions. See 'Products & Services' (Appendix D). Also a WordPress blog.

Blogs

Equality by Lot: The blog of the Kleroterians Academic and practitioner discussion, maintained by Yoram Gat. This group also has a Facebook page.

Video

90 minute lecture on sortition from Athens to today – by Étienne Chouard, in French with English subtitles.

Other Websites

Center for Deliberative Democracy (Stanford University) devoted to research about democracy and public opinion obtained through Deliberative Polling®.

Center for Wise Democracy (Seattle, Washington) has developed a set of social innovations that can facilitate the necessary thoughtful conversation of all.

The Center for Voting and Democracy FairVote is a catalyst for reforming our elections to respect every vote and every voice through bold approaches to increase voter turnout, meaningful ballot choices and fair representation.

The Deliberative Democracy Consortium The mission of the Consortium is to bring together practitioners and researchers to support and foster the nascent, broad-based movement to promote and institutionalize deliberative democracy at all levels of governance in the United States and around the world.

The National Coalition for Dialogue and Deliberation The National Coalition for Dialogue & Deliberation (NCDD) promotes the use of dialogue, deliberation, and other innovative group processes

The New Democracy Foundation (Australia) pursues alternatives more likely to identify common ground, return representatives to a focus on issues rather than opinion polls, and bring an end to the 'continuous campaign.'

Random.org has intriguing information about *true* versus *pseudo* randomness. The site provides a random number generator, games, gambling, widgets and more.

Appendix B

BIBLIOGRAPHY

<u>Reading List and comments from Terry Bouricius</u>
terryb@burlingtontelecom.net

Sortition: Theory and Practice, edited by Oliver Dowlen and Gil Delannoi (2010). A collection of academic papers from a Paris conference.

When the People Speak: Deliberative Democracy and Public Consultation, by James S. Fishkin (2009). This is the latest of Fishkin's books that discuss a system combining polling with deliberation among random samples of citizens. While not sortition as such, he proposes this system using similar reasoning.

The Political Potential of Sortition: a study of the random selection of citizens for public office, by Oliver Dowlen (2008). Dowlen primarily focuses on the a-rational, or "blind break" of random selection, where removing choice from human decision enhances a sense of fairness or protection from corruption. Much of the book deals with the details of the use of random selection in Italian city republics of the 16th century.

Saving Democracy: A Plan for Real Representation in America, by Kevin O'Leary (2006). Random sampling to form a virtual legislature is a major element of his plan.

Deliberative Democracy In America: A Proposal For A Popular Branch Of Government, by Ethan J. Leib (2005). Leib sets forth a proposal for a new branch of government using sortition.

By Popular Demand: Revitalizing Representative Democracy Through Deliberative Elections, by John Gastil (2000). Gastil deals with a concept related to sortition within and electoral framework, specifically, a randomly selected policy body in each congressional district, comprising a virtual third chamber.

Random Selection in Politics by Lyn Carson & Brian Martin (1999). Carson and Martin cover both historical and possible future uses of random selection and sortition in politics. They include sortition for representative bodies.

Random Justice: On Lotteries and Legal Decision-Making, by Neil Duxbury (1999). While touching on sortition and lottery voting (selecting random ballots to form a proportionally representative body), the focus of the book is the use of chance in legal decisions rather than selecting officials.

Toward an Ethic of Citizenship: Creating a Culture of Democracy for the 21st Century by William Dustin (2000). Dustin discusses many aspects of citizenship and extends the concept of the jury to the legislative realm as well.

The Principles of Representative Government by Bernard Manin (1997). Manin traces the history of election and sortition with regards to aristocracy and democracy, with keen insights into the thinking of the framers of the U.S. constitution.

The Voice of the People: Public Opinion and Democracy, by James Fishkin (1995). Fishkin primarily deals with advisory deliberative polling and policy juries (which he essentially invented).

Justice by Lottery, by Barbara Goodwin (1992, 2005). Goodwin takes a broader view of the social justice and equality possibilities of lottery distribution of public goods, but also touches on the use of lottery voting (selecting random ballots to create a representative legislature).

44

Is democracy possible? The alternative to electoral politics by John Burnheim, (1985). Burnheim discusses the shortcomings of liberal democracy and the possibility of a non-electoral democracy, which he terms "demarchy."

A People's Parliament by Keith Sutherland. (2008). Focused on the UK mostly. His plan proposes one chamber (Commons) be selected by lot to pass judgment on laws proposed by an elected chamber.

The Athenian Option: Radical Reform for the House of Lords, by Anthony Barnett and Peter Carty (1998), also obviously geared to the U.K audience. It was revised in 2008.

A Citizen Legislature, A Modest Proposal for the Random Selection of Legislators by Ernest Callenbach and Michael Phillips (1985). Using a point by point description and defense of their proposal for a bicameral legislature at the state and national level in which one chamber is selected by sortition. This was re-released in 2008, with a companion book aimed at the United Kingdom audience.

Additional

Stone, Peter, *The Luck of the Draw: The Role of Lotteries in Decision-Making* (2011). "An elegant and ultimately compelling book about the virtues of random selection in a wide range of contexts." – Geoffrey Brennan, Australian National University

Duval, Jared, *Next Generation Democracy: What the Open-Source Revolution Means for Power, Politics and Change* (2011)

APPENDIX C

STRATEGY

You may want to gather people together to discuss, plan and implement ideas. In which case you'll want to know:

HOW TO LEAD A WORKSHOP / SEMINAR / HOUSE PARTY

> 1.)   Arrange seating to facilitate interaction; encourage people who don't know each other to sit together; if appropriate, provide food
> 2.)   Watch "The Common Lot" video (30 minutes) or the "Next Step for Democracy" slide show (7 minutes)
> 3.)   Divide into small groups. Each group selects a facilitator and a note taker. Discuss for an agreed time limit.
> 4.)   Re-convene and report back from small group discussions.
> 5.)   Develop plans for how to 'make democracy real'

For step 3, the small groups might be assigned, or self-assign, particular aspects of the topic. For instance, they could imagine a plan to use sortition in:

City Council

County School Board

The board of a non-profit

State legislature

Or they could choose a broader topic such as:

What strategy overall would you recommend to further more equitable democracy? Locally, regionally, nationally (choose one or all, depending on time)

How should an individual or group dedicated to 'making democracy real' generate necessary income?

Aspects the breakout group discussions may want consider:

How would you set up a random sortition selection process?

What qualifications would you require for selectees: age? literacy? job experience? military service? citizenship in US? IQ score? police record? physical and mental health record?

Would you set term limits for offices? How?

What about using parliamentary rules of order for a legislative body? Who selects them? How are parliamentarians selected and monitored for performance?

How would you periodically access overall success or failure of a sortitionally generated assembly?

What procedures would be used for bringing bills/ordinances before assembly?

How would a sortitionally-selected assembly inform the public of its actions, positions, deliberations, studies, reports, and issues? Would representatives vote in secret or would votes be open to the public? [Consider that secret balloting could protect against the influence of lobbyists.] Would certain information be classified?

What limitations, if any, might be placed on executive or judicial power under a sortitional system?

Would a sortitional system be able to improve transparency, efficiency, and accountability for budgetary processes, income, spending, military preparedness and performance, environmental regulation, health, foreign policy, law enforcement, and public health?

How could a workshop actually incorporate sortition in its workings? For inspiration, see http://www.random.org.

This workshop format was originally formulated by John Sellers <sellejohn@gmail.com> for the Reading-Berks (Pennsylvania) Teach-In Series.

APPENDIX D:

Products and Services

Common Lot Productions

Inquire at <info@thecommonlot.com>

Available electronically

***The Common Lot*, screenplay:** Magical-realist comic provocation about the fight for the initial establishment of a sortitionally-chosen legislature. 136 pages.

> *One of the most intellectually stimulating scripts I've read in a long time.*

> *Both the Tea Party and the Occupy Movement could find this concept appealing.*

> — Lyn Vaus, Screenwriter, *Next Stop Wonderland*

***The Common Lot: Take-Off,* novel** (first of a projected trilogy): Linear narrative, follows two characters in the first Citizen Legislature. 225 pages.

"Interview from the Year 2030", essay: Looks backward at how the Citizen Legislature was accomplished. 16 pages

6'40" slide show: "Next Step for Democracy: A Government BY The People"

Half-hour video docudrama, interviews & meditations

80-minute video polished rough cut feature: docudrama, interviews & meditations.

<u>Hard copy only</u>

***The Common Lot*, novel:** Character study and speculative narrative about six people sortitionally-selected to be in the first Citizen Legislature. 360 pages

***The Common Lot*, novelization** of screenplay, 171 pages. (Available on Amazon.)

<u>Also:</u> Available for in-person **workshops, forum, performance, <u>classes</u>.**

<u>Other internet</u>

- Facebook page <http://www.facebook.com/CommonLot>
- Blog on WordPress <http://commonlot.wordpress.com/>
- Contributor to Equality-by-Lot blog <http://equalitybylot.wordpress.com/>
- Twitter: @CommonLotProd

<u>Four screenplays</u> (see <u>Amazon</u> "Author Central: David Grant"):

- *The Fight for Random*
- *Random Takes Off*
- *Democracy at Random*
- *Random Takes Baltimore*

About David Grant

David Grant brings more than four decades of dedication to political and community affairs. After obtaining a Master of Fine Arts from the U of Iowa's Writer's Workshop he became a producer-director for public television. Thereafter followed: self-sufficient homesteader; Peace Corps agroforester with upland aboriginals; executive director of community organizing group specializing in "The Listening Project"; founder of "Peace Troupe" (nonviolent action through the cultural arts); nonviolence educator and trainer for the International Fellowship of Reconciliation; and a director of Nonviolent Peaceforce providing unarmed protection of civilians in war zones. David is founder and president of Common Lot Productions

[i] http://www.opensecrets.org/bigpicture/reelect.php

[ii] See the chart displaying a few blatant discrepancies between the membership of Congress and the general population in the slide show: "Next Step for Democracy: A Government by the People". That chart is based on Congressional Research Service http://www.senate.gov/reference/resources/pdf/R41647.pdf (the URL does not load; must cut and paste)

[iii] Ole Worm's cabinet of curiosities, from *Museum Wormianum*, 1655. Original source from: Smithsonian Institution Libraries. Public domain.
[iv] Most systems of proportional representation are linked to political parties. None use sortitional selection. See http://en.wikipedia.org/wiki/Proportional_representation#List_of_countries_using_proportional_representation

[v] See Wikipedia's extensive list of voting systems.

[vi] http://www.cartercenter.org/peace/democracy/des.html

[vii] The Lenormant Relief, from the Athenian Acropolis, depicting the rowers of an *aphract* Athenian trireme, ca. 410 BC. Found in 1852, it is one of the main pictorial testaments to the layout of the trireme. SOME RIGHTS RESERVED

[viii] The Athenian democracy was at first restricted to particular property classes. By the middle of the 5th century BCE, the restriction was no longer enforced.

[ix] Scene of olive-gathering by young people. Attic black-figured neck-amphora, ca. 520 BC. From Vulci, Italy. Public domain. In British Museum.

[x] Big Foot's camp after Battle of Wounded Knee; U.S. soldiers amid scattered debris of camp" Contains at least 3 bodies in foreground, possibly four. 1 photographic print : albumen ; 9 x 11 in. Wikipedia: Wounded Knee Aftermath. Public domain.

[xi] Hansen, Mogens Herman, "Direct Democracy" in *The Tradition of Ancient Greek Democracy and its Important for Modern Democracy* (2005), p. 45-46.

[xii] Collection: A. D. White Architectural Photographs, Cornell University Library. Accession Number: 15/5/3090.00024. Title: Pynx. Photograph date: ca. 1865-ca. 1895 6th BC-4th BC. / This image, which was originally posted to *Flickr.com*, was uploaded to Wikipedia Commons using Flickr upload bot

on 14:22, 13 July 2009 (UTC) by Jpc4031 (talk). On that date it was licensed under

^{xiii} Wikipedia, "Pynx"

^{xiv} From Terry Bourcious (Equality-by-Lot blog): "According to M. H. Hansen, the show of hands were estimated by a committee of nine selected by lot for the day from among the Council of 500. If there was doubt (and even a single citizen could make the appeal), the show of hands would be repeated. Presumably, if the committee of nine was divided about the result, they would vote among themselves (thus the number nine rather than the customary ten of most small bodies of magistrates. Hansen suggests there is no record of voting dispute."

^{xv} Hansen, p 48.

^{xvi} *The Death of* Socrates, Jacque-Louis David (1787). Public domain.

^{xvii} Hansen, p 58-59. "The connection between peace and democracy has been claimed not only by neoconservative hawks but also by direct democratic doves…. examples, however, show that this version of the theory cannot be upheld…. a whole people can be as militant and bent on war as a ruling elite or a monarch…"

^{xviii} 6,000 of the approximately 30,000 eligible citizen voters

^{xix} Kagan, Donald, *Thucydides: The Reinvention of History* (2009), "Was Periclean Athens a Democracy?" p 98-114

^{xx} A sort of professional staff assisted some of those positions. Hansen: notes, p 65: "Important aspect of Athenian democracy…: (d) the separation of initiative and decision, so that initiative and preparation of all bills was left to highly active and sometimes even semi-professional citizens collaborating with members of the council of 500, whereas decision was what was expected from the ordinary citizens."

^{xxi} Hansen, p. 49.

^{xxii} Wikipedia "Doge of Venice" cites "Electing the Doge of Venice: Analysis of a 13th Century Protocol" "http://www.hpl.hp.com/techreports/2007/HPL-2007-28R1.pdf. See also Wikipedia "Signoria of Florence".

[xxiii] Hansen, p. 21: "…the first attested provision that regular town meetings be held was made in Cambridge, Mass. In December 1632."

[xxiv] Examples of independent discovery and invention include:
20th Century
* the airplane by the Wright Brothers and by Alberto Santos Dumont
* Polio vaccine by Hilary Koprowski, Jonas Salk, Albert Sabin.
* Discovery of the accelerating expansion of the universe through observations of distant supernovae by Saul Perlmutter, Adam G. Riess and Brian P. Schmidt
19th Century
* Typewriting machines by several individuals in England and in America
* The steamboat by Fulton, Jouffroy, Rumsey, Stevens and Symmington.
* Early versions of the bicycle by J.N. Niepce and Karl von Drais
* First practical gasoline-powered automobile by Carl Benz and Gottlieb Daimler
* The theory of evolution of species by Charles Darwin and Alfred Russel Wallace
* Electrical telegraph by Charles Wheatstone and Samuel F.B. Morse
* the telephone by Elisha Gray and Alexander Graham Bell
* the phonograph by Charles Cros and Thomas Edison
18th Century
* discovery of oxygen by Carl Wilhelm Scheele, Joseph Priestley, Antoine Lavoisier and others, 18th Century
17th Century
* formulation of calculus by Isaac Newton, Gottfried Wilhelm Leibniz and others

[xxv] Public domain

[xxvi] One of the questions from the pre-2008 naturalization test of the U.S. Citizenship and Immigration Services was: "What is the most important right granted to U.S. citizens?" The answer was: "The right to vote."
In the current test (2012) there are two questions about voting.
* "What is one responsibility that is only for United States citizens?" Either of two answers is acceptable: *"A: serve on a jury; A: vote"*
    * "What are two rights only for United States citizens?" Any of these four are acceptable: "A: apply for a federal job; A: vote; A: run for office; A: carry a U.S. passport."

[xxvii] Aristotle, *Politics*, 4.1294be

[xxviii] Differences between the south and the north reflected geographic and religious affiliations. Slave-holding Anglican Virginia plantation owners

won major constitutional concessions from individualist Puritan Massachusetts small farmers and merchants. See Woodard, Colin, *American Nations: A History of the Eleven Rival Regional Cultures of North America(2011).* From correspondence with Tom Timmins (Haydenville, MA 01039).

[xxix] Montesquieu, *De l'Espirt des* Lois [1748], Book II, ch. 2 as cited in Manin, Bernard *The Principles of Representative Government*, (1997), p. 70-71.

[xxx] Illustration of The Whiskey Rebellion, 1791. Public domain

[xxxi] See for instance: Federalist No. 10 (by Madison).

[xxxii] Extensively explained in Manin, Bernard, *The principles of Representative Government,*1997.

[xxxiii] Emblematic of Locke's influence upon the American Founding Fathers is this statement by Thomas Jefferson: "Bacon, Locke and Newtown ... I consider them as the three greatest men that have ever lived, without any exception, and as having laid the foundation of those superstructures which have been raised in the Physical and Moral sciences". The Letters of Thomas Jefferson: 1743–1826 Bacon, Locke, and Newton".

[xxxiv] Hamilton's rejoinder to the Anti-federalist argument (Federalist no. 35, para 9)

[xxxv] http://press-pubs.uchicago.edu/founders/documents/v1ch15s61.html This view accepting, promoting and devising plan to ensure a 'natural aristocracy' permeates deliberations and assumptions of even the most 'democratic' of constitutional framers. See, e.g., J. Wilson, speech of December 4, 1987, cited in Manin, Bernard, p. 118.

[xxxvi] One exception was Thomas Paine in 1792 when he published *Rights of Man* as a rejoinder to Edmund Burke's *Reflections on the French Revolution* (1790). He admired Athenian democracy and wrote: "What Athens was in miniature, America will be in magnitude." (Paine (1792) . [Footnote 34 in Hansen, Mogens Herman, *The Tradition of Ancient Greek Democracy and its Importance for Modern Democracy* (Copenhagen 2005).]

[xxxvii] The definition of 'representative' as the exact opposite of 'democratic' thoroughly prevailed from the time of the Roman Senate until the Jacksonian democracy. See Hansen, p 14-15, 25-29; and Manin. p 202-203 "Election of representatives."

56

xxxviii Photo by Carla Tavares (contact: Nuno Tavares), 

xxxix Hansen, p 15.

xl See Roper, J. 1898 *Democracy and its Critics: Anglo-American Democratic Thought in the Nineteenth Century* (p 54-55) From Mogens, p. 34. / The ancient Greeks did not consciously employ the concept of 'representation.'

xli Gienapp, William E., *The Origins of the Republican Party, 1852-1856* (1982) Chapter on "The Second Party System".

xlii Phillips, Michael, "New Age Doctrine is Out to Lunch on Three Issues". *CoEvolution Quarterly*, (Summer, 1980). Print.
Callenbach, Ernest and Phillips, Michael, *Citizen Legislature* (1985) and Sutherland, Keith, *A People's Parliament* (2008).
Note that "Citizen Legislature" in this article has nothing to do with the "Citizen Legislature Act" currently pending in Congress, at http://www.house.gov/house/Contract/termlimd.txt

xliii http://usgovinfo.about.com/blinstst.htm

xliv The 2011 GMAC Insurance National Drivers Test found that that 36.9 million U.S. residents failed the 20-question, multiple-choice test with a score lower than 70% correct.
As of December 2011, 93% pass the Naturalization test for citizenship.

xlv See Dowlen, Oliver *The Political Potential of Sortition: a study of the random selection of citizens for public office* (2008).

xlvi Confer Surowiecki, James, *The Wisdom of Crowds* for empirical evidence that diversity of views for non-technical matters always trumps 'the experts.'
See also Fishkin, James, *When the People Speak: Deliberative Democracy and Public Consultation* (2011). Working from The Center for Deliberative Democracy at Stanford University Fishkin demonstrates that when 'ordinary citizens' are given the time and resources to seriously deliberate, their solutions are wise.
Other apposite citations include: Page, Scott, *The Difference: How the Power of Diversity Creates Better Groups Firms, Schools, and Societies (2008);* Tetlock, Philip, *Expert Political Judgment: How Good Is it? How Can We Know? (2006);* and Sunstein, Cass, *Why Societies Need Dissent (2005).*

[xlvii] *"Women hold up half the sky"* is a Chinese adage, taken here to mean that all humans, irrespective of gender, contribute to universal well-being.

[xlviii] See discussion on Equality by Lot blog.

[xlix] Public domain, by NASA

[l] http://cdd.stanford.edu/research/

[li] Surowiecki

[lii] See "Group Think" in Wikipedia. Examples of group think listed there include Pearl Harbor; the Bay of Pigs; the collapse of SwissAir.

[liii] Sunstein, Cass, *Why Societies Need Dissent* (2005) and http://www.physorg.com/news/2011-12-knowledge-power-uninformed-vital-democracy.html

[liv] Confer The Center for Deliberative Democracy. They lead extensive deliberations of policy advisory groups selected through random sampling.

[lv] Manin, p. 109 "The concepts of 'likeness,' 'resemblance,' 'closeness,' and the idea that representation should be a 'true picture' of the people constantly keep recurring in the writings and speeches of the Anti-Federalists."

[lvi] Willem J. Jefferson corruption case in Wikipedia: Cash found in freezer at Washington, D.C. home of Congressman William J. Jefferson of Louisiana. This photo was entered Wednesday 8 July 2009 as evidence showing what was seized on Aug. 3, 2005, from the freezer of the Washington home of then-Rep. William Jefferson, D-New Orleans. Jurors in the bribery trial of Jefferson, who lost his re-election bid last year, saw photos of the infamous frozen cash. It was wrapped in $10,000 increments and concealed in boxes of Pillsbury pie crust and Boca burgers.
This work is in the **public domain** in the United States because it is a work of the United States Federal Government under the terms of Title 17, Chapter 1, Section 105 of the US Code.

[lvii] Silverstein, Ken, "Congress: The most dangerous neighborhood in America," *Harper's*, September 2007, http://harpers.org/archive/2007/09/hbc-90001300 and http://www.crewsmostcorrupt.org/mostcorrupt. The end of the article reads: *" … this is back-of-the-envelope stuff, and sure, to some extent we're comparing apples and oranges—members of Congress did not commit any rapes or murders, at least not any that we know about. But the fact*

remains—Congress is one of the most criminal places in America."

[lviii] See interview with former Congressman James W. Symington in "The Common Lot: Part 1" video.

[lix] See comments on Washington's Farewell address in Elkins, Stanley and McKitrick, Eric, *The Age of Federalism*, p 491-2.

James Madison, credited as "Father of the Constitution," famously warned: "A pure Democracy…can admit of no cure for the mischiefs of faction…such Democracies have ever been found incompatible with personal security, or the rights of property…" *The Federalist* number 10 (p 61)

[lx] The term 'voice equality' formulated by Gail Milissa Grant, the author's sister.

[lxi] "Interview with Dr. Donald Kraybill", video

[lxii] Johnson, Steven, *Emergence: The Connected Lives of Ants, Brains, Cities, and Software* (2002)

[lxiii] John Locke formulated 'life, liberty and the pursuit of property.' Whether Jefferson modified this phrase from Locke in the Declaration of Independence is in dispute.

[lxiv] For example, the chances are about one out of 100,000 that in a sortitional selection of an equal population of men and women the selection would be as out of kilter as 40% of one and 60% of the other.

The mathematical proof for the Law of Large Numbers was not established until the 17th Century. The idea of using sortition for representational purposes could not have existed with any certainty prior.

[lxv] http://thecommonlot.com/node/56 explains the mathematical calculation.

See http://www.random.org/ for intriguing information about *true* versus *pseudo* randomness. The site provides a random number generator, games, gambling, widgets and more.

[lxvi] Stone money at Hibiya Park, Tokyo. Public domain

[lxvii] Today's median household income is about $50,000. http://quickfacts.census.gov/qfd/states/00000.html

[lxviii] Since 1967, Federal law has required that House Members be elected from single-member-districts, thereby not permitting the use of proportional representation. U.S. Code TITLE 2.>CHAPTER 1>§ 7

[lxix] http://www.salaries.wa.gov/

[lxx] http://healthydemocracyoregon.org/citizens-initiative-review

[lxxi] Fishkin, James, blog.
What's Next California demonstrates how the people can take control of the agenda for direct democracy.
[lxxii] In British Columbia of the original stratified sample of 23,034 only 1,715 opted to be selected, 964 (4% of the original sample) came to the selection meeting and 158 were randomly selected.
See http://equalitybylot.wordpress.com/2012/03/21/allotted-assembly-for-budget-planning-in-the-city-of-canada-bay-australia/ - comments

[lxxiii] See Wikipedia, **single transferable vote.**
[lxxiv] See discussion at
http://equalitybylot.wordpress.com/2012/03/21/allotted-assembly-for-budget-planning-in-the-city-of-canada-bay-australia/#comments. See also:
http://www.newdemocracy.com.au/

[lxxv] Sortition is often used in awarding prizes. For examples, see
http://www.conallboyle.com/ExsCurrent.html.
[lxxvi] Hansen, p. 46.

[lxxvii] Personal communication with the meditation group, Three Treasures of the Pacific Northwest.

[lxxviii] Wikipedia, "Sortition", examples.

[lxxix] from http://equalitybylot.wordpress.com/:
"It turns out that the maximum size of a group at which personal relationships are still possible has been termed 'Dunbar's number', after British anthropologist Robin Dunbar, who theorized that this limit is a direct function of relative neocortex size, and that this in turn limits group size … the limit imposed by neocortical processing capacity is simply on the number of individuals with whom a stable inter-personal relationship can be maintained.
According to Wikipedia, the value of Dunbar's number has been estimated to be in the range of 100 to 290. Importantly, Dunbar's number depends on factors such as the proportion of time spent on maintaining the social

60

relationship. Dunbar estimated that a group of 150 people would have to spend 40% of its time on maintaining personal relationships."

[lxxx] Private correspondence with Rolf Carriere r_carriere@hotmail.com, retired UN civil servant. Also see "Cosmopolitan Democracy" in Wikipedia.

[lxxxi] Thanks especially to Terry Bouricius at http://equalitybylot.wordpress.com/2011/12/14/which-actors-for-each-activity/ - comment-2476

[lxxxii] Sutherland, Keith, *A People's Parliament* (2008)

[lxxxiii] For ongoing discussion about strategies to implement sortition see http://equalitybylot.wordpress.com/2011/12/20/strategies-to-implement-sortition/ and http://equalitybylot.wordpress.com/2010/08/05/institutional-design-power-parameters/

[lxxxiv] Huizinga, Johan, *Homo Ludens: A Study of the Play-Element in Culture*, (1938)

[lxxxv] Common Lot Productions at http://thecommonlot.com/node/42

[lxxxvi] "Network" (1976) directed by Sidney Lumet, written by Paddy Chayefsky. The actor Peter Finch playing "Howard Beale" makes the appeal.